No Basis in Reality

No Basis in Reality

Rob Nixon

Copyright ©2018 Rob Nixon
All rights reserved
ISBN-13: 978-1-7327842-1-5
September 2018

Listed

When it's dark thoroughly,
I sometimes listen to the low rumble overhead.
Inside, light emitting diodes,
other people being served,
not one connection between them and me.
There are tree frogs in my neighborhood.
And at night they constantly croak
until they stop.
Their defense, sudden silence after racket.
They make you hear your footsteps
and absorb every crack.
Predators arise at night too, and I can hear them
mixed with their all concerning, focused laughter.
Fuck.
I am a mess.
Condoms litter the streets.
So cold on a night like this,
not a strand of DNA is left.
I am there too,
I join them,
but conscious on the cold ground,
and hidden from view.

Caught in the Dark Web

I clicked on a video.
Very professionally made.
Good for a reason,
little to distract from the message
that was about to be delivered.
It is no different than a clean sheet of

parchment and the best quill penmanship.
The following is extracted from my notes.
The whole floor—
I see cubes lined in queues,
one section is oriented in a certain direction
and then another on a different grid,
and so many workstations in each,
and still another grid,
all on an ice blue carpet.
I would say 400 people work in this place.
Even though they close,
a few cubicle doors stay open.
They probably stay open all night.
There is absolutely no sound.
At least I don't remember any.
(My mind was trending on the tracking of the shot,
the tour, how it was done,
and how it was edited.)
An office comes into view (not a corner office).
The camera descends,
and there is a man inside,
perfectly dressed and fully made up,
seated behind a desk.
The perimeter office doors
which encircle the workstations
and grids are all closed except this one.
It is daytime.
"Subliminal audio communication
consists incidentally of liminal notes.
These will be heard distinctly by the subject
and it will be irritating.
It has been described as a bell-like sonic covering

No Basis in Reality

of pitches and trills.
Your subject will perspire.
You have two things against you then,
the primitive state opened so and agitated.
In desperation to decipher your message,
unmistakably to him or her,
the human mind will over-the-border borrow
from its dream world,
suspicions of reality—
basic building blocks to make sense
of the cheap wind chimes' clamor.
A complex deep thought,
almost Tinkertoy-like in abstraction
(not a hundred-piece exaggeration,
but a few pieces anyway),
will incorporate your message.
Your target will self-diagnose.
Most will be unsuitable.
I know my business.
But I try informal covert rehab visits
for my throwaways.
I hope you do the same.
Many are blessed with enlightenment.
A nice counterweight to the raving schizophrenics
roaming the streets.
Neither of these are useful to government though.
It is in the business of exploiting the psychology
of the suggestible vast majority in between."
I think I am an abandoned building,
gutted,
it is the cold air.
I feel it like snow during the day.

It is constant. I feel I am susceptible
to the thought that words unreasoned
and reasoned are spoken at once.
It's a language expressed in nouns,
the other parts of speech, groans.

I Won't

I doubt I suffer from an abnormal psychology.
If that is your diagnosis, I want a second opinion.
Consider why the strange,
as in foreign, unnerves us.
That we would all like to know.

Remains

As a guest in a private cellar,
I am told I am loved because I am a beautiful,
and that I have made myself so,
that I'd never needed an escort,
that I knew instinctively the social path to take.
Possessed by these thoughts, though,
I feel not let go.
I feel also bound to return to society—
matured and ripened.
This overgrown rough of humanity,
itself putrid and flourishing,
yellow and green,
I am tossed back into,
as from a passing van.

Can I Put That Another Way?

You work in the theater,
so, you've been around artists.
(Who knows? Maybe you haven't.)
Listen, if someone misinterprets a piece,
the artist may correct,
but he or she (mostly) could not care less.
There is a high and low for transcendent
understanding in the human species,
and almost every artist knows that.
Even those on the periphery can be reached.
God will be jealous, conjuring up figures.
But that's where we always fall.
It is our snare.

Oddly Soft and Rounded

I can appreciate the altitude,
the depth of the cliff,
the protuberances—
how Pachinko Palace-like
one must fall,
not tumbling far enough
or fast enough
to the next broken bone
or obliterated tooth
to die,
but live on to the next
(still the next!)
awkward
angle
impact.

Radio

I am a country song at 3 am
in Midlands, Texas, 1973.
The light in the window of the house
that can only be seen by looking across
the back alley is a cancer diagnosis.
It will be an average harvest this fall.

Criminal Thoughts

You think I have good taste, right?
Well, I am totally digging your face right now.
I think you're so pretty. And you must work out,
you're lying, you have such a nice body.
I am totally into that too. You are sexy to me.
And I like looking at you. I know we are not
seeing each other, like that, you know, dating,
but I think it's really cool we're riding the bus
together so much. I like sitting next to you,
and talking with you, and smiling, and feeling good.

Exhalation

My innocence is spoiled.
Confirmed, as you get older and sicker,
you're pushed further and further
out into the margins, and you die
in dirt. There's hardly anything
that can be done about this.
Some people understand this.
I have talks with those who do.
"Let's set that aside for thirty minutes.

There are other things.
I'd like to discuss them with you."
If we were there in the forest,
we would be pulling nits out of ourselves.

Banquet Room

Outside a just slightly ajar exit door,
this unmicrophoned voice infused the walls,
and nestled in with the central air,
and the isolation of the corridor
still under construction,
one night when I was taking my break.
"I told you all that I was looking for more,
and gave you other hints at my intentions.
Admittedly, I was not too specific about anything.
But I thought it better than a sudden resignation
and an announcement of a new position elsewhere.
I don't know why I told you these things,
and thought these things,
but here we are.
I'd be lying if I said I wasn't curious
about the construct of all this—
the unseen mental forces at play—
especially the ones that aren't discovered yet,
let alone described.
The skeleton of it is raw emotions.
I avoid them, at least outside in the real world I do.
So, I was impelled, for lack of a better word,
to do this little team-building
to avoid the teary sentimentality.
And I recruited and enrolled you to my project,

to my cause—
leaving.
It wasn't easy for me to concede
that it would be too hard to tell you all good-bye,
to say that to each and everyone one of you.
That is a lot of farewells.
That is an emotional thing.
I didn't believe I could do it.
So, while I don't have the knowledge
to explain it all more precisely,
I knew somehow that I needed your help.
I needed the collective."
Meanwhile, what a world—
Professor Hartengale's head is in her hands
in the sink inside the single-use restroom.
I hear weeping.
"I spoke earlier to a colleague of all of ours,
a doctor of psychiatry.
She mentioned that there seemed a lot
of joy behind my smile.
I said that I was overjoyed, yes.
Only the day before, though,
I had felt spasms of grief. She said,
'The extreme manifestations
of sadness and joy,
that the healthy individual experiences
changing,
leaving,
is absolutely selected into the species.
Fresh memory of these extremes
will put the new normal into perspective.'
That reassurance—I hope those two words

are emphasized enough—
that basic psychological fact
expressed, reasoned,
and delivered so therapeutically,
was a narcotic.
Bull's eye.
But you all want to know why I am happy
too, I suppose. That really is a surprising question.
And to think that it comes from a society
which lives by the ideal that happiness
should be self-defined
as long as it does not impinge
upon the health or well-being of another.
But I will answer you.
For a lot of us,
work life is one thing,
but personal life is completely different.
I know different people in both.
To let someone in is extremely rare.
I think many of you believe the same.
I find it hard to accept only seeing the opposite
of myself in this regard; for the very people
I would want to present themselves to me
with openness on this subject
have this selfsame reasonable view of things—
they stay away.
Others come close.
We are safe,
but this kind of isolation is terrible.
I want to say sometimes,
'You are totally a person I would let in.'
But I don't.

There is a mournful quality to work life now,
and the hubris of it has been pointed out to me.
I am very motivated to put that feeling behind me,
and I am almost there.
That is why I am happy."

Apple

Dark, overwhelming conscience—
identity card and propaganda broadcast at hand.

Sweet and Sour

Heaven forbid me trying to
change the way you think, let alone feel.
I can only hope to convince you
that just like the sadness that is always about you,
another emotion can constantly be there too.

Seventies Drama

I know I'll seem stiff trying to
keep us both dry, holding a not
quite big enough umbrella above
our heads.
You and I have both
seen similar scenes,
and they are uncomfortably charming.
You and I on film would be no different.
In a long shot
we would not recognize ourselves—
our gaits unnatural, faces overshadowed,
forms obscured. "Is it really? No.

We are tending together!"
I'm sure my eyes would give me away though.
Up close, it would my search-for-recognition face.
In uncomfortable situations, I always look that way.
And my smile would give me away more
if I found someone.
But no, no one.
The dialog would be yours,
and I alone would hear what you think.
Also because no one else you know
is around in this downpour.
Our scanning eyes though—
as we walk
a pace,
a pace,
and a pace-and-a-half,
halting at lights—
search for a face.
But no face.
A green,
and we walk,
and we enter,
dry from the rain.

Career

I know there is happiness; I feel
joy right now.
It is mixed with sadness though.
I have felt mighty dumb lately.
If it wasn't so hard to understand,
the accomplishment wouldn't be there.

So this is really going to happen.
I will be tendered an offer
and I will accept.

Darkness May Interrupt the Day

I don't think people realize what truly
committed groups of people can get done.
And how brutal it can be, especially
when it fits the definition of illegal
in every sense except that which takes
the broader view of things in mind.
There is war, too, in addition to all that.
The inspiration behind the
crime that must be done
is shamanistic.
I hear the words
and the woodwinds.
Night quiets them.
That concerns me.

Bull's Eye?

It has this in common with art,
one of these comes first,
perfect aim or force of the blow.
But you are not out in the open,
painted red, soaked, ingrained.

Never Really Again

Peekaboo, here I am. One see for you.
Worth mentioning, though, is the feeling

of trust, a little bit to the side of
where in the psyche we are talking about.
They share the same bit of anchorage.
This is fortunate, because one thing easily
remembered is when totally betrayed.
That is all the way to the surface.
That neural pathway stays plaque-free.
It fries with crystal clarity what to
never do again.

It's Just a Place

When you say you are protecting
your property, you mean money.
You may think you could get
a lot more than I can possibly
afford in this market for this.
But I look at it this way,
if every single unit is being
rented out at roughly what
I am paying, the profit margin
here is shockingly high already.
Because, let's face it,
what I am being provided
here in return for my hard
earned money is hardly worth it.

Induced Coma

You are an engineer.
You pack exactly what you need,
medicine, clothes, toiletries,
everything.

You are supplied thoroughly.
Your car surpasses all safety standards.
Things aren't going to get in the way.
You are going to experience quality
the good things
completely.
It is practiced.
Like an artist, it is now instinctual.
When you enter a room,
you have that entry planned
so that the maximum amount of ambience
can be absorbed by you.
You sound it like an instrument.
You bow across the bass of it.
You learn the mysteries of the places you haunt.
I think you have done that to me.

Sounding

You have a sublime mind.
I know we have intelligent conversation,
but it still qualifies as light.
For some reason,
I appeal to you.
I know it's not love.
It must be a feeling I can hardly imagine.
Every day I cherish that you appreciate me.

Doug the Troll

That man who interrupted us
(it had to be a man)
in our chat forum,

he was a dog who ran
into our house,
snarled and bared his teeth,
growled and barked,
and then took a dump.
He left his excrement behind—
scroll up and you'll see
his steaming pile of wit.

Pastels

I feel I'm in the DVD Extra
part of my life, right now.
Bonus footage!
Bonus footage!

My Fault

I'm afraid I try to be indispensable at work.
I'm sorry for what that makes me look like,
I guess.
I am totally locked in on survival.
There is no leeway for me—
no brother-in-law, cousin, or good friend
that would be there for me.
Don't be snotty. It may not be great,
I think it is.
I wish more people felt like this
to be honest.

Human Beings Are So Violent

Reason states that it is to one's advantage

for everyone else to die. On top of evolution
at last, because clearly the opposite is innate.
The rough boys haze instead of kill each other.
That appeals to this inner nature.
Murder appeals to reason.

It Must Be Morning

Well, I would have thought
somebody would have noticed,
and said, "Let's give a little bit back to him."
I don't think an apology is good enough.
I know *forgive*,
but I think that was for the brethren.
Delivering from evil
isn't even on the verge of forgiveness.

Yawn

I don't dream anymore.
I fear euphoria is slipping away.
I will put it to the test, tonight.
Will I sleep walk then?
Aghast, I may.

Unstoppable

Ouzawa, it is impossible.
You cannot go over and correct him.
My God! In front of his family?
And he cannot function,
so, forget that.
That twelve-year old who saw you,

saw your soft brush against yourself
(just that once)
as you thought of your university boy—
he believed he was willing you to do that.
He perceived correctly the pleasure on your face
before your hand even moved.
"Female," he commanded…
How can this be corrected?
Here is what will happen, most likely: His family
will wake him from his fantasy,
and he will hate them instantly and forever; focusing
that energy into scholastic
achievement and physical fitness,
and of course, conquests,
he will live out the ideal existence of a viral man.
Ouzawa, you must stop this.

Bit Much

The nastiness of infection I understand completely.
I do not want to be infected.
It is low on my priorities, though,
because I honestly think people go mad
if it's too big a deal.

Nestled

And to that special one I go home with in the forest,
to home—
to home and away and to home all the time, there is
sameness everywhere but there.
There is also the sense of the many.
But that thought is for the lost.

(I like to share secrets with you
as we hike through there.)

Meeting

My eyes, my ears, everything,
it all tells me that this is supposed
to be about honesty and truth.
It isn't.
It makes me feel at ease, though,
when I hear that this is not business either.
What else could it be then?
A dialogue.
Geez.

Twitter

The authorities did not order this.
They do not like things like this at all.
To script a name, and an inciter of the mob,
is their only involvement.
The stoning itself takes but six seconds,
and all scatter in borrowed coats.
How does anyone know,
except the one who holds the coats?

The Song Unflocked Birds Sing

But no, it was an auditory illusion.
Just a call and no answer.
An unknowing, positive, hormonal rebuke
in response to a vacuum.
It sounded like a child's *lolly* on the beach.

Streetwise birds ignore novelties of sound.
Cities clank out new ones all day long.
I did not hear a reply.
This invader was completely and utterly ignored.
(I've already forgotten the fiend's song.)

Simultaneously

Strutting across the carpet
is so close to walking, every step,
while swallowing every surface.
Which is what you want; the stream which buoys you
and moves you
also slides sustenance up into your gullet.

Her

And it truly is a team approach.
It's the standard outpatient mental
health facility for the most part.
There are added touches and accents.
These are provided by the faculty,
and passed down to the staff—
real world therapy fresh from the lab.
I meet with the doctor once a month.
She gives me insights into psychological
forces as I lay out for her portions of
my thinking and emotions.
She recommends a lifestyle change.
There must be strong evidence
that the psychological forces mentioned
here have laws associated with them
that require a willful act

in order to tap into them.
And the nurses give me my shots
that let the buildings pass by on either
side of me. And I don't think about
all the nasty, sweaty people inside of them,
nor the people all around me going nowhere,
except for the ones following me, and coming
out of the buildings looking at me.
I just go around to all the places I go to.
And remember people and what they are like.
All the staff are here to keep me going to my other
appointments—getting my colonoscopy,
my physicals, dentist, and eye doctor.
When I go to the lounge to chat with friends
and avoid enemies, I'm sure the eyes, ears
and noses are the doctor's as well.

It's Prismatic

If there was any design to all this,
then it was orchestrated by Jehovah.
I think we as artist just have a highly
nuanced communication gene.

Today

Common civility is just that,
base, barely making it.
Anyone who strives for that as a personal goal
exposes himself or herself as uncivilized.
And as a dream for society,
a revelation of a current low opinion of it.
It is a lowly, base existence.

Only being intelligible as a good thing
when viewed in retrospect as that environment
from which real virtue tends to flourish.
The thought is to encourage it
as nitrogen for the garden.
Uncommon civility is rare,
but strived for, provoking it forward,
the way it should be. Not even common
civility is seen much anymore.

Always

Leave. Your tolerance is draining.
Your feeling toward me can better
and more accurately be described as hatred.
We just bumped into each other.
Let's look at it that way.
We are incandescent lights in that way, too,
flaring up brightly the rest of the kilowatt hours.
That is your smiles and well-wishes,
they are overwhelming me,
and I am out.

Cascade

I think there are an awful lot
of people who live in dread
every single day of their lives.
I think the area of the psyche where we care
wastes each time one thing of importance
is replaced by another.
There is a difference in the possibilities,
a downward trend.

This is dread, getting used to that.

Retirement

Alerting someone that they might
be less than ten years from a
lucrative retirement (if looked
at favorably and in the right circumstances),
seems the wrong thing to do.

Wittenberg

If you ever vowed to have your looks
never determine how you were treated
by excelling at everything,
to prove yourself to each and every person
that you would ever meet in your entire life
after the ugly truth of this society
could no longer be disputed (probably at fourteen),
then you have done well and achieved success.
Society's Zeus,
horrifying each successive generation
in a new and weaker way until
a break is made,
and a new story is told, and a new deity is born.
The new god or goddess breaths less tangibly,
but transcendence itself going forward,
immortal.

Rehearsal

However I have come to be
in this position, I am here, and so

are you,
so I am going for broke.
I was thinking,
maybe the two of us,
although total and complete individuals,
grown up similarly,
having similar temperaments,
(would get along as siblings),
could gather a little bit of trust together
and pour ourselves into each other,
give it one last pathetic try.
How fun an idea I think it is,
even as it is natural
and not framed,
still ideal.

From Scratch

You were raised to see things scientifically,
to discard the impossible.
Your life was impossible, so you discarded it.

It Runs Out

For the next twenty years?
I don't know if you've noticed,
but I can be a pretty competitive guy.
The world has gone crazy.
I plan to show the world how it's done.
I see the esthetic in the mosaic.
Five stars, real is cool.
But all the death?
Not just direct casualties alone,

it's genocide as it's always been.
And all the screeching?
I could do without that too.
It won't be hard to beat that.
We will be better than cool.
Ok, the plan is to make a good deal of money
while things are still relatively atrocity free—
to be very blessed sparrows.
To escape with our lives and American dollars,
when things get worse,
and retire in Spain,
getting a tan,
and being inspired constantly,
not wanting to count how much is left
in the treasure chest
when reaching in for more.

Horror

We'll need things in those days,
when we're sixty,
and you're still fine.
We will have to be like
Abraham and Sarah in Egypt.
We will experience
the world's masterpiece of horror.
The only other act going on.
We will reimagine it.
It will be splendid.
We'll come and go and
be protected in our trespasses.

P.S. (Password Protected)

It all sounds so wonderful.
I hope that I am conveying
how joyful this thought is making me.
Don't think about the end of civilization.
Think about being apart,
being uncivilized; that is what
is making me happy.

The Seaweed Solution

Sigmund, please tell me a fable.
Christine's dad is telling me about
his toxic mix to clean out the colon.
(It is not the 22nd century.)
Now he is telling me of all the -ectomies
his friends have had,
and the -ostomy.
How pieces of colon get taken
out of good people every day.
I imagined a concoction that expands
like some foam insulation sprays do,
filling up the large intestine
and all its crevices, and all its bends,
pushing out slowly,
wiping out the foreign bacteria,
bursting and devouring the polyps,
while searing and cauterizing the wounds.
Now he's talking about shitting.
Diet and nature was his spiel—
how the gut is delicate in respect to foreign matter,
to avoid it.

"Let the colon do
exactly what it was designed to do.
Move at the correct systolic pace."
This man is not an enterologist.
And he needs to open his eyes.
Abject humanity is a scavenger.
That trait evolved with our intelligence.
It dominates everyone's family tree.
Going back so far,
and only branched off so recently,
that whatever the fuck you think your pedigree is,
that is what you are too.
No one's going to feast on my bones just yet either—
if that was this father's intention.
I'll have to go read up on it.

I Am Not Responsible

I will not be induced
by ideas hidden behind words.
There is not much future for me.
Deaths come so frequently now,
mine would just be another.
That threat has lost its potency.
So something so imperative on pain of it,
might not be.
I might be thinking a bit clearer
on this type of thing now.
There might not be causality.
Thus, I just plod along, living,
slowly dying, unsusceptible.

Woo Who

I probably have less a plan than you.
I could propose a plan that we can both
be a part of though. We agree to have
a pizza and a beer; and don't think
you would break my heart
to make it the last time, I fully understand the
high probability of it being our only meeting.
"Amongst a better class of men…"
I take very little offense at that.
And deep down, in this situation,
you will find me highly in agreement.
But for that length of time
that we are there together,
I have a girlfriend,
at least to all the men and women who are there.
That would be totally worth it.
I have confidence that it won't distract
me from helping you have a good time too.
I will say something like I have index cards
full of topics, because it is charming
and I'm good guy. Don't drink too much.
I can't erase my flaws, I don't think alcohol
would help to get rid of them either.
All of us have two visions of the future,
one is the end or goal, the other is the steps
in between. The latter is the better way to
proceed, but it is the child of the former.
This will show through. Look at the architect
at the construction site. He or she will back
up a few paces and not see what is there.
I hope I don't, but I'm sure I will,

go blank a bit and perceive
a feeling which does not exist.
Now that you're on notice, though,
that husbandry is at work,
a feeling of *Dang!* should squelch
the impulse to laugh, and just produce
an enigmatic smile, which will only
encourage more reverie in me—
and so on. That is the way these thing work.

Bad Thoughts

I can make it that way too.
What must you think of me?
A meat-eating beast,
who hasn't even fathered one single child!
Born into the privileged race—
in an exploding, burgeoning city,
full of culture and strength,
a magnet for any who have a
touch of class or even wit,
a historic city for the future to romanticize—
and you made it only to the lowest of low class!
A feeling of fear comes over me,
when I think to the condition a human might fall.
I pray for my children.

Enteroctopus Dofleini

Seattle, you need to seriously
figure this shit out. If this were
an amusement park, it would
be totally un-go-able—too crowded,

no security, and nobody that
works there seems to know anything,
Getting there is a problem too.

Psychology

You know what I think the
wrong thing to do is? To scoff
at an -ism that is ten generations
thick. You get instant disrespect—
work with that. Good luck!
The patient will never allow you to operate.
A referral is your only hope to not cause
an end to the patient-doctor relationship
permanently.

Duality

I can't help thinking about the original stimulus.
That movement which caused
this rolling stone to be coated
with us living things. "Trust me. Go this way.
Time has proven me right. I live, don't I?
The wrong die." So spiders spin webs.
We're just along for the ride.

Another Style

I guess I took it too seriously,
when I read The Stranger's,
"Welcome to Seattle, New Person."
I'm all like, "Well, I'm sure you all
don't want to grow the population any more,

if anything, the opposite. So, um,
who do you want to leave?"
And you're all like, "Um, you."
And I'm all like, "Ga."
And you're all like, "Ya."
And I'm all like, "See ya."
And you're all like, "Good riddance."
"Bastard(s)."

Every Situation

Nothing in this field is black and white.
If you allow yourself to become frustrated,
it will only hinder you from getting things done.
You have to ask questions,
analyze the options,
use logic,
use common sense,
and decide which answer
will work best in a given scenario.

Cool With It

If being super nice
has made a few people suffer,
I guess in comparison,
it is still totally worth it.
And I think almost everyone would agree.

And I Know You

I ate late last night,
so I dreamed.

I dreamed of you.
I am happy right now
thinking of how happy you seemed.
It must have had something to do
with the outdoors, and sun, and art.
If not all at once,
then together in their closest proximity.

All Day

I want to feel the scent of you again
on my shin.
Impression, caresses.

Two People

Modern green,
missing button,
pink shirt,
purple ink,
purple number two (smaller).
Shark skin,
little long,
blue Stafford
(too long!),
silver tie.

The Night Provokes All

A hermit, forty-eight years in silence,
even he would talk to another.
He would come out and say to anyone,
"Hey man, how's it going? You seeing this?"

Representing

I will lose.
I fight against the truth,
so I must be a lie.
The liar invents realities,
so do I. And shares it with those
he loves—guilty.
The liar is a coward. The comparison
isn't exact.
I fight against the full force of it every day.
That is tough.
Archers wound the nobility in the rear.

I Feel Good (Better Hide Now)

That's the respect I feel for each
and every one of you. I think
it's obvious now that the
feeling in mutual. Individual
respect—that dynamic—one-on-one
is the only true respect there is.
Popularity better captures any other
innocent misapplication of
the word, *coercion* less innocently.
A wave of feeling truly is
triggered by these lesser imitations.
It can peak.
I present as evidence, popular revolution
and the police state so often in the same lifetime.

Principles

And, "Fifth," will be the answer
to the tolling of the bell.
The health council has determined
another outbreak is occurring.
"Besiegers bemused by this Mass communication!
We will not surrender!
Haughty crows! Immune, you outnumber us!
Without us, you are the lowest on the chain,
until, winnowed away like us, you are last eaten!"

From the Mach-Men

Big Brother corrected in his last enclave,
are you the last one free of the thought crimes,
or do you still organize?

101

Yeah, I suppose I am unique
in that I think
beautiful skin should not be
exposed to excessive heat
in the shower.
Does body temperature on body
seem so farfetched?
I think it is obvious.

Buzz

There is a simple thought that is in total harmony
with the impulses of the technology we are using—
here and there are one.
This voice line through which we converse,

which emerges at each of our ends
exclusive and apart (one would hope),
is part of a fiber optic network underground
that doesn't get used much anymore.
Some kind of heart somewhere is being deprived
of its blood. The electromagnetism of our love
being transmitted so clearly is proof of this.
A lonely call across a dry town is transmitted so.
These thoughts are so privately ours.
And nothing in organic existence needs to try them.
Parapsychology explains the rest, or noetics.
They eliminate all other existence
and physical laws,
leaving just the subject and the object.
Tantric dance is not irrelevant,
distance is, so is time.
Cause and effect has been compressed.
Discredited?
Nevertheless, it has settled into my head,
and that knowledge is also being transmitted,
and it's being done at virtual speed.
I think it is transcendental.
I think it is an enhancement.
Let's throw a little shade into our connection—
remote-view, meet on the astral plane, channel.

Cold and Very Warm

As you remember, I was talking with
Jerry when you just walked in to work.
He handed me over to you to say hi.
You sounded well but sad.

No Basis in Reality

It was when
we were having those wildfires in Canada.
I told you that you sounded congested.
You said you had a little cold.
The only other part of our
conversation that I remember
concerned the solar eclipse.
You had made an eclipse viewer
out of a family-sized cereal box
that only one other person tested out.
I remember that you didn't sound sad anymore.
We hadn't really communicated much after that.
I think only one small e-mail exchange.
It was around Thanksgiving
when I considered you
in connection with this thing.
I remembered your Christmas cards,
how you made them personally,
and that I didn't ever get you anything.
I remembered how much it meant to you
to arrange for potlucks for birthdays
and when someone was moving on.
And how disinterested everyone else seemed to be,
especially me.
Later on,
you seemed to be becoming disinterested too.
On your department's last day here,
I didn't really want to go up there to see you off.
It was near the end of 2017
and it was late at night
when I felt guilty about who I am.
I've lived so long with

the never-get-too-far-involved philosophy,
that it's become a part of me.
I think the essential manifestation of it is that there
are a lot more things that I am ambivalent about
than probably most people are.
It is hardly a positive state of mind
(i.e., designed to cause a reaction in a relationship),
it is totally passive
(as in oblivious to possible reactions); so I don't
remember any look on your face,
nor was I ever conscious
of any emotional reaction on your part at all.
So, you sounded sad on the phone.
It had been about a year
since you had deliberately gone out of your way
to do something really nice and thoughtful for me.
I thought I might try to return the favor.
I thought about the things about that past year
that make me sad,
and what possibly could be causing it in you—
I thought about me,
I thought about another year in my fifties,
I thought about the doctor, mental health,
I thought about Cheerios boxes, manners,
and President Donald J. Trump.
A card, I thought, I will give her a card.
That is totally appropriate.
If she is sad, I think it will make her happy,
and it can't possibly cause offense,
You told me once,
that of the art you like,
a part of your appreciation goes toward found art.

No Basis in Reality

You said you peered through the dirty glass
of a nondescript building you passed by once.
There was art going on in there.
My memory is foggy on the details of what you
described to me after you went inside.
But I'm pretty sure
it combined the visual arts with sound.
I can't remember how.
That's probably because
it didn't really make sense to me at the time.
Trying to piece it together logically, though,
I imagine it had something to do with sound waves
producing visible, physical art.
But I have an independent memory of metalwork, too,
so I don't know.
Another time you told me about
music records pressed on x-ray film.
I think you said you heard about it on NPR.
As I said, by the end of our conversation,
you didn't sound sad anymore.
That impression has stayed with me.
The thought that I was responsible for it
made me feel good.
I don't feel good about too many things these days.
Even if the impression wasn't true
and I was deluding myself,
it was a worthwhile fantasy—
a noble emotion felt for another human being,
a completely pure thing,
and nothing to be ashamed of.
I looked in the Word templates
for Thanksgiving Day cards, but there were none.

Ultimately, I found
a fall-foliage-decorative-border menu template.
That would do.
8½ by 11 too.
Then I looked for a funny turkey picture
in an image search.
Even though you're a notorious turkey monster,
a photograph of a real one
was out of the question—so not cool.
So, I just picked
the first cartoon of one that was listed,
and wasn't trademarked or anything,
and I pasted that within the borders of the menu.
I added the sentiment
as font sensitive as I cared to get.
I made the theme, as it's called,
a very muted, almost brown, blue.
It didn't really matter, as long as it wasn't purple.
Anyway, I thought it went well
with the orangey drawing and border.
The first part of the text
I sized comfortably readable,
the rest of the line, "EVER",
would fill the rest of the text space.
I hoped the space would be big.
That was my thinking behind the thing.
And I wanted the maximum amount
of pleasure received by you,
with the least amount of effort on my part.
That didn't come out right—
improv,
ad lib,

flash art.

You to Me

You walk in your bones,
and that is style,
which is superficial,
but incorporates art.

Spotter

Blessed with a gray spark of reason,
that inner black and white medullary core
can be convinced on and off.
The one felicitous aftereffect
when you injured your back,
was your research into safe sex positions,
just in case—
because, you know, the gorilla.
That breached the wall and catalyzed
the neurotransmitter. I thank God
every day that you discovered
McNerney's Position.

Wound

The basic emotions are there, but neurotic.
We were loosed as individuals,
at a certain time—
as free from conditioning and biology
as we were ever going to get.
Progressively the laces are re-tightened
into a most exquisite knot.

Exquisite, meaning beauty or flawlessness,
and knot, meaning twisted.
That is what surrounds the individual now.

Greased Pig

What's it all about, then?
If you're asking me, I think it's
about meeting someone for the
first time, someone in trouble,
a person for whom your whole training
in life has been directed,
and for whom you have put out your
open for business sign—
if possible, this person is to be helped.
If this treatment gets beyond the willful self,
sometimes the client will experience truth.
You are a reasoned person.
What billions of people are prepared to reveal
to you will not be reasoned.
It will either be what your profession likes to call
magical thinking,
or a cover story, so far from the truth that story
is the only good word for it.
Layered on this, patients sometime only reveal
what they think will get them help,
and what they believe the doctor wants to hear.
That's the focus of such a
person going into the encounter.
The patient has prevented therapy.
Diluted so, it can only be coded a hydration.
You are in the same role

as an athletic trainer treating cramps.
This person is often the most appreciative too.
That is the last cruel trick of this patient's will.

And Sweat

As one gets older, the urge to
sound like others almost completely
disappears—
seen,
heard,
enough.
I sit on my beach then,
on a sunny day,
three,
a slice of watermelon
far too big for my head,
high,
disarmingly sweet, seeds and all,
devouring.

Vacay

Gonna have a break,
going to treat myself right.
Gonna have a lie down,
every tissue at ease,
best 'script for disease.
All cells in static—ecstatic.
A different beat now—just be—
want to always be.
That's the beat now—just written down.
Okay, so not total rest (written down?)—

but moderation!
No dogmatism in rest for God's sake!
Body wants to stay with me,
not going to die,
mind's finding words for immortality.
Stressors? A multitude,
most unseen around,
but there,
everywhere,
unaware.
The hairs on my head,
jellyfish feelers,
protecting and feeding—
say hello to my ego.
Brain needs a break,
needs a stress enema.
Gonna be good as new.

The Mach-Men

When the doctors ask for one of these
[pointing to itself]
to do something—
they are under the impression such subjects will—
it will be done with class.
I do not understand it at all
in comparison to the medical doctors.
Nothing.
I just apprehend.

Warning

The questioning of brotherly love grows—

we've been checked before on this.
I don't think we want a second coming.
Please! It would be a massacre.

Seriously?

So, you have had lunch with men
at work before, one-on-one?
And none of them at the end of that
pleasant hour said to you,
"I know it's wrong to say this to
you on the job and everything, but
I have such an urge to kiss you right now"?
We've known each other long earlier
than when you came to work here.
Women know when a guy is really into them,
instantly. And you know a lot of guys
are really into you—a lot!
You should have a professional
do your makeup. Only making
what's already really good even better.
They will tell you
that they sculpt some not so pretty faces
into something presentable, every day.
Their art, though, is only
fully expressed on worthy landscapes,
a la Frank Lloyd Wright.
It's only temporary. They know it.
It's kind of artificial. But all art is.
They would look forward to working with you.
If it never went further than this—
me telling you all this—

epically failing in the workplace—
I would totally be okay with that.
Well, maybe not.
But I hope it gets across
how good the thing is in my mind.

Coherence in Cars

Thumping beats,
cautious mirrors,
waxed and dirty,
right turn, left lane,
direct and fast,
and not.

Fooled

Everyone must recoil at the thought of joining
the mob, not just me.
It is just raw, tribal, brutal
instinct that makes the child
join in with the bullying crowd—
hating it instantly and throughout.
Unable to break the grip of the group, though,
the child acts the monster to give us
(meaning anyone witnessing the spectacle)
shape for this demon. But still apart,
sane and reasonable, the child remains.
The child thinks, "I don't like being forced.
I hate this." Despite well-meaning teaching
to the contrary, the child will always believe
that bullies win, and that the self is vulnerable.
People who believe otherwise are wrong.

Jewel

Egypt says,
"We have assumed an apex,
geometrically up from dirt,
at the top we shall find it,
revealed by mathematics."
Fasting away in India,
"Nirvana is ascension.
Successfully fade into the stars,
while miners suffocate,
far below their own land."

Wacky

It is the uniqueness to blend in that I dislike.
I take my cues from those around me, instead,
whom I respect. I think that's natural
in a chromosomal sense.
I agree with you when it goes too far though.
When someone imitates, it annoys me too.
Your new creation of individuality
is sold out utterly, though, with bigotry.
You can only accept variety
in things like fashion
and not opinion.
And, as you age, I cringe.

My Guys Are So Real They Need Haircuts

I think you can, in a closed vessel,
become a soul. A sad face in your paintings
showed me that. To represent to humanity

one must be available to be possessed by it.
Ironically, being too social prevents this—
or at least loving it too much does.
You'll find if you treat society as a chore,
the impressions it makes upon you,
while primitive, will be much clearer.
Irritation seeps in especially for me.
You'll be more naïve, but if you stick
to what you know is true, the combinations
are all out there for you.
Only loneliness can be expressed
with the opposite style of life.
Call it a sad poem,
they sound abandoned to me,
It is a toy poodle on a work day.
"Oh, I will express myself,
if only to fill the emptiness."

Clear Answer

So, what? Do you think I'm lying?
You think I'm just making this up?
So, tell me, what is the truth, then?
It ain't that.

Petty

Is this the part
where I am supposed to say,
"Not one dime," and you
laugh out and say that's all
everyone says?
Congratulations! You found

a weakness to exploit. How
brave a fighter you are.
I really don't see the likes
of you and I
strutting shield and sword out
to face each other
in combat. Your words to me,
boldly boasting of your skills
and the glory with which
you will be bronzed.
And I don't see myself, frankly,
roundly condemning you.
And boasting of my crown in heaven.
We are two people on the wrong page.

Again?

How hideous it would be to be forced to move.
Have to look for another hole.
To hide until it's light.

A Spot

I know I should be ashamed of myself.
But at the very least, I am flesh and blood,
even if a total actor personality, not the real me,
I am a functioning human being.
Beelzebub himself couldn't cough up
a familiar as charming and pleasing as I can be.
Everything you want, I am your total mark.
Well, almost everything. I will correct
what needs to be corrected
when my darling errs.

There I would be, to be wrong in that situation.
I think the specter is that purely, I am organic.
Emotions outside this dynamic
can be felt by me also.
It's snowing in Seattle right now,
February 21st, 2018.
Tomorrow is Thursday,
my Friday,
four-day weekend!
Monday off too.
I am taking lunch with you tomorrow.
I guess this is the real test, right?
Snow day!
Seattle will look so romantic covered in snow—
I'm coming to work. It is too good to waste!
I recommend you send me that e-mail first thing:
"Sorry. Couldn't make it in.
Next week!
I really want to try!"
This day simply must be spent
with a rugged gentleman.
His overcoat must cost at least a thousand dollars.
A big mittened hand must hold yours.
The crunching of the ice underneath your boots
will be so rhythmic and sexy.
You cannot waste it on me.
Or you could wait five years for another chance.
The usual happened, a sunny and cold date.
By two, most of the snow was gone.
I hope I matched the sky in clarity.
I am not very good
at expressing myself coherently in conversation,

but I think I got across the idea that,
of the complete pie chart of social ability,
I was occupied in a position
that required proficiency
in only one percent.
I did it well—serving with class.
One percent is just that.
The rest, I guess, was a mystery.
So, I tried to subtly relay the fact
that I am a complete dud in all the rest.
"Maybe it helped you through your work day.
It would not enhance your private life in the least."
That is paraphrased what I was trying to convey,
with turns in the conversation.
I could not spit that out explicitly,
but I thought it would have been obvious
that the two of us have nothing in common.
It cannot exist.
Somewhere there appears the valley,
sun behind the ridge, moon not quite ascended,
sensible for its darkness,
standing out in the vista,
seen from the veranda.
All the eye widens to fill this chasm.
"I want to commune with you.
Go places with you. Reason things out.
I like the way you've chosen black
as your dominant color.
You've found your place in this world,
and it is an honorable position.
So have I.
This is what we must do:

Follow the dark corners,
don't go mad,
do things that need to get done,
be free and follow direction.
We share a studio, so to speak.
I like your light green beret,
it makes everything underneath darker.
I hope I inspire you, too, to escape from it all,
and go to work in our real vocation,
because I am a devotee."

Tube

Backward and forward, finally knocked off,
and ground up under hooves in the dirt,
the cowboy goes down.
Again, I replay.
They should wear helmets.
I should wear a helmet.

I Don't Miss It

"I think you were here just long enough
to see Mary leave."
Then I relayed like a parrot,
that some nice guy out there
is supporting her while she goes back to school—
an idea that fits in quite nicely
in my brain's architecture,
one that will survive rumor
and become factual.
I think I miss and even forget
much more interesting

true things that happen to people.

Badass Haiku/Kanji

    Edgar Allan Poe:
"Quoth the raven, 'Nevermore.'"
    And nothing further.

The Deeper Meaning of It

Okay, so our worlds weren't painted
by the same artist,
but of all people, I thought you might appreciate
the thought of a silly online computer course,
its completion,
and resultant joy.

Disturbing Scenes

My most traumatic trivialities
were the times when I was put down
as being not part of the crowd.
It seems that feeling has a very central
position in my psyche.
Probably a lot of ancient emotions
are in that part of psyche too.
Since the situation is avoided almost
to the point of phobia, the feeling
hasn't aged well in ignorance and isolation.
It is not me, but it pre-defines me.
I know the image I present,

and the problems it causes with others.
Remember, I have been one of the people involved
in all of my relationships.
My mind is still sharp, and I have a good memory.
I am not delusional.
I don't want to feel that way.
But *so don't* doesn't work.
Some still think that I can change.
God bless them.

Neutral

I would think a clinical psychologist
would understand the concept
that, in its extremist form,
self-consciousness can be the complete
isolation of the individual socially.
No need for culture, business,
interesting friends, or sophistication.
I know those are desirable things for you.
Pocatello?

Mach-Man Love Letter

You can totally tell some random friend,
whom I would have no way of knowing,
this suggestion from me,
for us
to have this life together.
I want to make you feel comfortable.
Tell this friend also
that I am a normal homo sapiens, physically,
civilized to a certain extent,

and that I want to mate with you.
I know this reads like a love letter to the aliens,
and I don't care if I offend with my language.
If frankness by me on this subject is seen by you
as a fault, I can only conclude that a superficial
relationship is all that is desired.
(But desired, nonetheless?)
Adding reason and intelligence
makes every emotion more human,
and therefore better.
I await your reply.

It's Not You, It's Me

It's been a long time now
in the pond,
and I've been compounding,
collecting,
complexing—
I wouldn't say evolving,
but to borrow from that analogy,
this line has died out.
I have given this society its last dance.
I am so humbled that I can live
a comfortable life though,
make no mistake about that.
I want to seriously thank you for that.
A few other things: That raise for me,
damn, I almost thought
I built this comfortable urban lifestyle myself,
it kept me in my place.
And thanks for constantly

being there to correct me.
I've known many times,
and thought I've been right all along,
but turned out I was wrong,
tone deaf wrong.
And for saving me—
really,
left on my own, I would surely have destroyed
myself by now, way too early.

Tomboy

You know what I was thinking
just now when you walked through that door?
I was thinking that is either Lindsey
or the second foxiest chick ever to come in here.
Are you kidding me!
How are you doing? Good to see you!
I had such a crush on you, oh my God,
You are so beautiful!

Pathetic

When the molten planetoid
is confirmed to strike—
is only months away,
don't expect anarchy.
What is the point?
I see brotherly love,
and virtue.

Oak Island

No Basis in Reality

The light just hits that red lighter right
in his breast pocket.
I can see the butane pulsating.
His cardiac muscle contracting
to momentarily suspend death.
It keeps flailing about in there,
suspended deep in his thoracic cavity.
Will it fail in its hundred ways?
Or another of his vitals,
will one of them begin the disaster?
I smell the tobacco. I see the stained fingers.
I listen to his story.
All the while keeping my good eye oriented
on his cardiac condition.
I bet he gets tired very easily.
His mind seems tired.
It seems he's always done a good job,
been loyal, had genuine good feelings
for almost everyone.
A high sense of duty was important to him.
How, if he hadn't found religion,
the whole thing would seem pointless.
He is flushed.
Nowadays, he says, he can't even
organize a game of solitaire.
"I think it's more than just instinctual," he says,
"the way I've tried to live my life.
There has to be some reason attached to it.
I don't have to apologize to anybody,
even those whose feelings I may have hurt,
which, most of the time, had something to do with
me not responding the way a normal person would.

I don't claim innocence for
my lapses in behavior (bedroom).
I only mean the general way
in which I have conducted myself
all the way and into the 21st century,
in the United States,
in this modern city."
Here we go.
"Some really rich woman has it.
The author and the Queen were supposed
to enjoy the poems and replies transiently
and then burn them.
Somehow, at least this one survived.
Even today it would be considered pornographic.
Word is, its authorship is patent by its quality.
The effect that age has had upon it,
not that it is deteriorating,
but the images it conjures in this day and age,
four hundred years later—
him, the Queen,
the thing becomes more powerful with time!"
The red butane is percolating violently.
"The man told me that all sense
of proprioception disappears.
He couldn't believe he remained standing,
or how his head and eyes kept moving.
He thought the effect was enhanced
by guards observing him read,
something they themselves weren't allowed to read.
But he reiterated the power of it was quite sufficient
without them being there.
The effect was an extreme unction.

I remember how old he looked when he told me.
I must look the same.
I really never quite understood
why he decided to tell me.
He had stressed the secrecy of it.
And now I tell you."

Four Stars

I've been evaluated at only 80 percent.
Even at 20 percent less than capacity,
I'm still better than all of you!
That is the truth!
I want to be perfect.
That grade bothers me. As we all know
that bother must be expressed.
It is worth mentioning.

Tweet

Venus armless, I am in your embrace.
A smile in a face so fair,
so incomprehensibly with me,
and incompatible with my cold, hard stare.
Sad.

Empty Space

We are usually only left with our fears
and our prejudices.
These, it seems,
are right at home where ourselves used to be.
Ending up a basket case or a bigot

may seem an all too fleshy viewpoint,
and way too—I don't know—American,
but that is my non-clinical experience.
It makes me sad too.
It makes me think about lost time and waste—
putting on a face and a personality
and thinking it's yours.

Immortal Honor

Let us be clear,
I think it should be about legacy now.
At your age, in your position,
what opportunities for honor and respect are left?
So few.
And mostly just chance occurrences.

Only So Far

Acknowledging arrested development,
you'll find me deferential on most things still.
Not down with the
Princess and the Pea-jazz though.
I am dirty and I'm not going to obsess about it.

Cold

I've heard some of you characters
find out who the crowd dislikes,
and then tell off that person in public.
You are twits.

Warmer

A lot of you play yourselves too.
I know that is not a new criticism,
but you are total divas about it!
I don't like the carnival.
Here's ten dollars,
leave me alone.
I'd rather not see your gallery, either,
or your new car.

Decaying

I am wasting time,
lying about.
What an affront to the architects of my genome.
Or are they jealous? Their fondest dream
realized so many years after oblivion?
I don't care.
That is pointless knowledge.

A Person Is Hands Typing

You're tripped up by your own logic.
You've discovered I'm selfish.
I readily admit it.
I was spoiled growing up.
Fortunately, I matured plain and poor.
So I was kind of forced into isolation,
ironically, to protect that selfishness.
This benefits both me and others.
And you want me to what?
To socialize?
First off,
I am totally unsophisticated and unknowledgeable

about fifty-year-old things.
My age group recoils with me
at the thought of a reconciliation.
What's more,
you all might not be aware of it,
but society is eddies, currents.
These forces are natural as hell,
but don't behave as physical forces do.
There is minimal effect of one to another.
Surfing through this is—well, it's awesome!
And it's someone who gets it!
Attuned to the rhythm of it,
divorced from consciousness—
that part of the mind totally focused
on the next move to make.
I am totally bad at that.
And how out of place I feel and adrift.
I must get in other people's way too.
I must cause friction with those incredulous
and those full of pity.
I think it's best for all concerned
if contact is limited.

Co-op

Pentothal.
"Live free.
That is for you.
Do not question the methods of the doctors.
You've seen the educational films—
they are required,
the ones you watch on day one of each grade—

age-appropriate discussion
of the two most important things in life,
sex and politics.
Let me tell you,
you know the stories you were told
about the troubled high schoolers
in the twentieth and twenty-first centuries?
How it was the cause of everything?
How observant young people
got their friends medical help?
How cool it is that it's been cured?
It hasn't.
It seems these humans can
hold their breaths a long time.
I will tell you explicitly.
The Mach-Men are for when they surface.
That is the one truth I can tell you.
You have eaten forbidden fruit.
Count the cops."

FU

O my god, this is the biggest FU
to everybody of all time!
FU everyone, everywhere!

Expressed

I bet we funked up the jungle big time.
There's a huge part of the brain
that couldn't wait for Pythagoras.
Unknown why.
Probably had something to do with mating.

Tiny

Overcome in adolescence.
Big noises like thunder
fourteen seconds away.

Wow

What a turnaround:
It's the right enamored with
a Russian autocrat, and the left leading
un-American activities investigations.

Mask

I always think it's funny to play ignorant,
to cover for my own jumbled and
continually debunked thoughts.
It is a dangerous society to be uppity in,
and my muse urges caution.

Very Unstable

This is one of those thoughts
that can only stay conscious for so long—
young, good-looking women
are not romantically interested in you
at all.
I like the idea that this thought is diving
into my bones, guiding my movements,
giving awkward signals everywhere—
loser.
These physical manifestations, then,
would be for my self-preservation—

instinctual acts.
The higher reasoned thoughts
sound something like—
it cannot be real,
keep your reason about you,
it is insane.

Unindicted

Convinced I am free (in a way),
leaves us face to face,
as over a backyard fence.
It will probably remain light.
That is enjoyable.
I am all for that.
I like deeper conversations too.
I think we can figure a lot of stuff out.
Time wears away the ugliness.
One day we'll meet outside in our bodies.
I will speak confidently to you,
because I know we are compatible,
and you will listen.
And you will tell me all about yourself
with the same kind of diction.
And I will fine tune mine in response.
We will be a duet,
because we each deserve it.

Annoyed

I would not be so bold
as to ask if you controlled these things,
but I would wonder if you could control them,

please!

Enemy

Why does everyone want me to experience
the world their way?
Whether it came upon me as the logical result
of cowardice and poor decision-making,
as an innate tendency,
or as considered decisions
(the third is correct),
I look at the world my way.
I like normality too.
I just don't like the group thing.
I think it encourages the worst kinds of behavior.

(Paranoid)

I see the controlled environment.
I see I'm the subject.
Intensive treatment is the salary?
Your time?
Don't worry about de-escalation; I understand
the concept of iatrogenic illness.
You will agree that my position is unique.
I am experiencing reality in a way
that you will never understand.
You can map my brain
and understand my psyche only so far.
I like seeing things the way I see them.
I don't really want to speculate
on the identities and choices of presentation.
I am sure it was all well-dosed.

But I think things like that are cruel.
The result was idiopathic.
If anything can be criticized,
it would be the background.
The initial assessment placed me within parameters.
Would I be a patient that would clearly benefit
from the findings of such a study?
I think you should re-classify me as *early*,
as in below basic, intermediate, and advanced,
as the new evaluation
of my motivation to known stimuli.
I think I require more intensive therapy
than the question here.
It was an interesting perspective, though,
being treated as a fifth grader and only in the third.
I guess that guy is gone forever.
Pity.
I think the approach was fine.
The failure rate in this science is very high.
You knew that coming in.
It is normative with willful disease.
One thing— I think I responded well with the
behavioral desensitization techniques.
The proper procedures to de-escalate anxiety
have been reinforced in me to my great benefit.
I will proceed on my way.

Godzilla

Ouzawa, the beast is sitting next to
you on the train. He is magnificent.

Activated

The brain invented this fantasy
under this amount of stress.
Its body demolished,
input blanked,
cellular destruction in progress,
connections in the mind are made at once.
Escape to a happy synapse.
A billion suddenly.
P.S. Shapes achieved.

Let Us Compare

I just saw one minute
of a thirties black-and-white.
I got myself into that Mountie's lodge,
heard the voices bouncing off the walls,
experienced the one concerned about the other,
and concerned about his girlfriend too.
I am watching the movie
and am all three.

Cubism

As in *The Hunter's Prayer*,
as I aim,
I am aimed at.
We are constrained in our shapes—
in relation to other shapes,
and in the whole,
and so out of proportion!
Why does that dead horse matter so much?

Nice Note

We set aside thirty minutes each week
just to chat—from light to heavy,
one hundred percent honest,
totally spontaneous,
except for your prepared cards.
I grew accustomed to it. Cheers!
Every day is in relation to Friday.
It is the climax.
It is the subject.

Fireworks Show

Some moments are the best.
And if I have to wait through other parts
to get to the next great moment,
so be it.
It's all good.
It booms like my heart.

Unique

I am securing in my mind
every impression in the past,
as you superimpose yourself
upon them in comparison.
It brings a smile to my face
seeing you thump around the house,
being with me.
I'm delirious.

Predators

Love hours in Utopia
and the molding of intellect,
gray clay.
It is the buzz of the Academy.

Taboo

I hate the word, the tone,
and the eeriness of it,
but sepia describes memories well,
really well.

Emotions Tangled

Ceremony,
torchlit,
worship,
sacrifice.

Stories

I love to hear how proud you are
of Reuben's wit, and how Nissa's so smart.
It is refreshing.
I just came from a place
where people would tell me things
they wouldn't tell their closest friends.
We (even including me) heard what people thought,
because they told us,
and because it would help make them better.
Medical doctors give them therapy in return.

Press

I'll stop asking about your hobbies, sorry.
You were an actress, right?
At one point?
I was just thinking with your looks,
your presence, your build,
at some point, someone would have tried
to open doors for you.
I don't mean that in the least to be salacious.
People trying to help their art by helping you.
They do exist.

Future-Speak

Let me get a little Eddie Haskell on you, Gladys.
There is a mixture of humanity.
We are a shattered mirror.
Not so easy to sing now for the City-State,
or organize rallies.
This has to end.

Hamartia

Hunters sense the universal hunger.
They feel it when they step out into the deep green.
They become an echo of what is not there,
they become a smell.
Evil hunts us.
Trapped down here with us,
every chance will be taken to despoil.

Served

This is not going to be one of those

competitive marriages, is it?
Each trying to be the alpha?
Well let me start off
by telling you that you hit the jackpot.
Realistically, you couldn't have done any better.
You're going to have hard time with me on that one.
Go ahead, your turn.

Snake Handler

I almost always get mistaken for someone better.
Let's face it, almost everyone is better.
Being a letdown doesn't really bother me anymore.
I was never really social.
I'm guessing it would have gotten old really fast
if I had been.
I would have willed myself
to prove all those people wrong—
whomever walked away from this man
feeling disappointed.
Being alone a lot of the time,
getting these reactions more parsed out,
is probably the main reason
I am immune to the shame of it.

Trained In

You are *so* not done with this life, are you?
Since fourteen, on your own, it is ingrained.
Little girl lost on Earth? Hell no.
Trained since childhood
progressively.
You have a strong mind that functions very well

in the midst of this chaos.
How unbelievably stupid some people are!
Parents bring up their own flesh and blood,
and stupid!
If you need money you go out and make it.
People are looking to team up
on the things all the time.
You go into every situation, and memorize
the dead ends, the landmarks, the turns, the stops.
And internalize rule one of networking,
keep your mouth shut.
You will always have a leg up on folks
who didn't learn this until college.
You got this.

Communique

We would be both embarrassed,
so let's just save it,
and chalk it up to impossibilities.
The feelings experienced in these group things,
generational things,
I am insensitive to.
That is considered a crime here.

Vulcan's Furnace

I was young when I remembered growing up.
Now, sometimes, it flashes across my mind
in the middle of a dream.
Surrealism jars into something
completely different—
the store, a street at six am, a school.

Then is no longer dormant.
Synaptic networks fire off in the bedlam.

Read This on Rainy Days

Let's talk about success.
It is an unstable element.
A short burst of existence,
fused briefly in an unimaginable universe—
when somebody wins a multimillion dollar lottery.

Damn Right I'm Intimidated

People that have been here the longest
know where I have been, know where I started.
In your heart, I know there is true egalitarianism—
love, honor and respect for everyone that you meet.
That is the general spirit of this organization too.
But I felt a little disrespected.
I was entrusted to care for
the health of our population,
although only superficially,
but in the most visible of ways.
I had to balance that
with the juggling of routine business,
whatever that happened to be that day,
at the County Hospital,
which is managed by one of the
largest universities in the United States.
Add to this the very trying circumstances
of homelessness, drug addiction, mental disease,
and the criminal culture.
"Good morning, Doctor!"

And being paid as the janitor—
for years.

Future Argument 1999!

Really?
I use too much water?
Whether I do or not is secondary to the gall.
Okay. Let's say I do.
And indeed, you might pay ten extra dollars
to the State every month.
For that, you are going to put me through this hell?
Of second guessing things
that are on normal subroutines?
I would have hoped for tolerance.

It's a Defensive Thing

We don't go into sealed rooms to discuss,
we do ten thousand other things simultaneously.
Some of that is inevitable, we're busy,
some of that stuff is allowed in on purpose, though,
just to dilute the attention.
This is done not so much to not hear the message,
it's just a way of judging the message
before receiving it.
It's a manners thing.
Because a lot of *are you serious?* exclamations
would reflexively leave our mouths
if we gave full attention to some of this shit.

Aching

Clear,
young,
bashful,
unashamed.

That's Why

That kind of intimacy is.
And there's always a sense of burden with it.
That is how one positively identifies it.
Primal instinct responds to this
as dread of being trespassed.
It is felt today, correctly, as sadness.
Things are really that impossible.

Exit Strategy

I have a fear of being trampled.
A perfectionist when it comes to reading moods
has no advantage over the novice
when it comes to stampedes.
Get to the exit.
For God's sake, mothers, carry your young!
It's just a matter of whom—
a statistic then.

Because Purple

I lust with reason.
But that quality is our peacock feathers, isn't it?
It gives carnal instincts color,
and acknowledges the hips.
It bounded me over to you,

and made me ask if you were single.
And I made you blush.
And getting a flattered, "Yes. But no,"
I said I noticed the weight you'd lost—
just found your figure attractive—
and if you were getting propositioned more.
And getting a flattered, "Yes. But no."
You know, getting that email at seven AM
the next morning,
saying you wanted to revisit the subject
we had discussed the day before,
made me think of those wildlife shows,
"The aggressive male has targeted a mate.
That mate has acknowledged the aggressive male."
When we met for lunch that next day,
that was our embrace.
"Try to guess what I'm going to say."
"I'm terrified. It can only be what terrifies you too.
You want to commence the process
toward a sexual relationship."
These declaratory statements are so necessary.
They enhance things so much.
But so unique in the universe,
that the unnaturalness of it can be jarring.
So you whispered.
I watched your figure as you walked away
from the table to get your knife and napkin,
and told you so.
You measured your words,
and asked about my STD status,
my politics,
and any potential romantic complications.

You took my word for two of those things.
I went and got tested for the other a few hours later.
We were just as nude then
as we were a week later on your bed.
"If we are going to do this thing,
I think I better introduce you to someone."
A stomach can feel so empty and full.
After I unburdened myself,
I teased you and said your smile was irresistible—
said we should be serious.
I think I know why you were smiling though.
One distinct part of your mind was saying,
"Ugh, men… it's always something,"
referring to my introversion.
While another was saying, "I'm so lucky."
Blended in anyone's head that produces a smile.
Mostly lucky is what I feel.
I usually temper that spirit with bitterness, though,
suspicion, jealousy, and eventually, depression.
The sounds of those thoughts
are what I dance to, unfortunately.
(That is not revealed.)
Instead, I told you truly that I loved you.
And I felt like a zombie.
As I did later on,
with my face buried
in between your shoulder and neck,
going at it way too hard,
but the sound of it keeping me sane.

Red Eye

Roughly translated:
"These full planes are so hard.
But I love it.
Non-stop, though, you know?
Inevitable, all the way to the ground."

Token Resistance

In a leaky vessel, with shots by me,
the avenger comes ashore.
That is all I know.
There aren't many left out there
that even know that.
I'll need all the luck there is.
All plans have tenuous components
that have to be accounted for
and re-accounted for.
But overdoing it makes whole plans vulnerable.
Psychopaths know when to execute.
It takes drills and training too—but that's the past.
Can't do anything about that. The future?
He owns that too.
That just leaves
the event horizon for me perpetually.
Another example of serendipity and justice,
so rare.

The Big Andowski

I know most of the bad manifestations of
relationships can be laid at the feet of men.
But the fallacy that the one hundred percent
honest exchange of feelings and ideas

leads to healthy fifty-fifty relationships
is almost always the female's delusion,
and always leads to very lopsided relationships.

Food Without a Face

I like vegetarian toes.
Something in the chemistry.
It is hard to decipher.
The word lovely comes to mind,
like a choreographed dance—
the taste is that good.
Not at all like the meat eaters' toes.
The difference can be noticed
everywhere on the body,
but most decidedly here.
The tongue likes the texture of your thighs too.
The striations and papillae
complement each other nicely.
As does the sweat pulsating out
when mixed with saliva.
I confess a special weakness, though,
for your flanks.
Inside, not baggage to be dragged around,
instead it is what propels you forward.
When I chew on this part of you,
which is also much firmer inside your skin,
I feel voltage discharging inside of my mouth.
I cannot determine what is missing,
when I go to your more tender parts,
or what is added.
There is this impression, though,

the little hairs on your torso
outward pointing,
as flavors of you are digested.

Lusty

I think you wanted the
most superficial of Muzak
in this nice elevator going up.
It somehow prolongs the ride.
And that we're sharing this car with such VIPs
is cool with me.
Because, although cramped and separated,
we are not alone.
We stare at each other
through thermals of perfumes,
and are so perfectly together.

I Am Too Tame

It still innervates the sinews of my feet.
But, overall, it is an unpleasant feeling for me.
Adrenaline just makes my whole body throb.
It doesn't paw me up the mountainside,
shove the knife in deep and eat raw.
It just gives me a headache.
I feel it in my loins too.
I don't think it's a companion twinge.
The most important part of the body
is aware of the situation and is producing
copious amount of testosterone
to help rectify the situation.
I just clench my fists.

Male Gaze

So how are you doing?
We seem to be in a black and white movie—
1965, with a blues/jazzy feel.
All doors don't shut right.
Some were poorly constructed,
and others for a million other reasons.
I have to double pull on mine hard,
as I feel and listen for the catch,
then gently key-turn to bolt the lock,
and I'm outside.
A woman walking a dog,
a boy and a wagon, singing,
the dog barking,
a postman—
back to the woman with the barking dog,
she is wearing white capris pants,
what difference what kind of top.
She's leering at the postman,
she also soberly discerns the *me*, alternatively.
The smile that stretches across her face
reveals that she's made
all the right decisions in life,
as she sniffs out her disapproval
to the subject/camera.
Every time the dirty glass door opens,
and the traffic sounds burst in,
the waitress looks.
She's friendly enough.
But I can read that it's not real.
I decide to tip her well,
if only to dismiss the pretense—

but that never works.
I'll look at her,
and look at her,
and in between ignore her.
Is there culture in Southern California?
Down by the river.
The bells clang above the sticking door,
and my wallflower turns to greet me—
always so shocked and disappointed.
I put on my apron and grab my broom.
I think I hang things right.
She never does though.
She actually volunteered to do it.
But there is nothing wrong with the way I do it.
Mrs. Krauss knows that.
And Mrs. Krauss also knows the mosquito
is far better off learning about the artists,
interpreting the works,
and selling.
She does that last part very well.
At this for eight years,
she can tell who's going to win any auction,
and at what price a piece will sell.
Her selling style is traditional/fabulous.
Mrs. Klauss wishes she'd be more morose about it.
And I agree.
I don't think either of us
can be very objective about it though.
Clearly, her manner is designed for the patron.
It is hardly a new concept.
But we find a shattered lordly image these days,
and we manage every little piece.

It gives the servant an incredible advantage.
I see you can turn it off immediately and control it.
You must imagine it though, Dolores!
When you're at home,
or when you're here and not on stage,
I bet you feel yourself
gliding around doing it, don't you?
Gleefully dancing around from patron to patron?

Myofascia

She hurt her back not far back.
An unexpected positive thing that came from that
is that I now understand
a little bit more about boundaries.
The idea of me rubbing, massaging,
kiss, kiss, kissing that hurt away
wasn't well thought out.
"I hardly know you.
Presuming to paw (and to even place your mouth!)
on this deep tissue injury of mine,
which is felt with every breath,
and is so slowly heeling,
shows a fundamental misunderstanding of affection.
It is starting to feel a little better.
(Although it may be my nervous system ignoring it—
which is not good. Scary.)
I am under the care of a physician—
a medical professional,
one whom I have chosen,
personally.
It hurts. Don't you understand?"

Inertia

Old Man and the Sea-like,
I am dying.
Even Freud knew it.

Organic

We are future dead things,
walking on bits of other dead things.
Like Star Trek said, we infest.
Variety? Magnificence?
One might as well admire
the mudslide that's about to kill you.
All that can be said
is that we flourish and mature
most spectacularly in this filth.
Ten billion years in the future,
if a small piece of this world
is studied by others so infesting,
they would discover our sequencing.
The Earth is the eyesore of the Universe right now.
And neither will ever be rid of us.

Welcoming Environment

What do I do when I'm alone?
I lounge about on the couch and
hang out with my living room—
which I paid for,
and which was not influenced in the least
by my friends' taste in style and décor.
I put it the way I wanted.

There is a little bit of clutter,
some things are a bit tricky,
and I'm sure there is a smell,
but that's all easily solvable.

Proofed

Your brain is full.
With your work life
making up a way
too high percentage
of your waking life,
and your other worthy pursuits,
the culture that you're a part of,
your age and experience—
you've filled it up to an extremely high
homo sapiens potential.

April

And as for depression,
it's pointless to go on about that.

Coping

As a matter of fact,
I do not have social anxiety.
I am actually very good at it.
I am incredibly charming.
I could calm myself down right now,
if I had to,
compose myself,
stop shaking,

get in that car,
maybe send it through the car wash,
go down and meet you somewhere,
and start our love affair.
I know that's the right thing to do.
And I know what the right things to say are too!
I am honest, have timing,
and I don't have any high expectations.
That makes me very witty.
And I am not dying either; I am not a fern.
I am going to live for a very long time.
Remember, that was the plan.
And so it was.
I'll just have to add you to it.
We'll have a blast.

Spoiler Alert

In case you missed it,
Chrisley farted on his show.

Not Lovelorn nor Hopeless

If you're looking for a personality
who belongs to organizations,
whose beliefs can be written about,
I am not him.
I am quite oblivious to the atrocities
going on around me. I just thought
you'd merely like to read something
I came up with. I am under the
impression that the ideas that
I am expressing are logical and reveal a deep

understanding of human emotions.
And that they are put together with cold, metered,
rhythmic words, that produce a sublime effect.
I have this feeling.
I was hoping that it was shared.
It is better if we know.
If a publisher reads something diligently,
and says that it is not good.
Says that he or she cannot imagine
anyone thinking it was.
And that the only saving grace for the author
is the idea that he or she wasn't really trying.
That would be hard to take.
But I would accept it.
I hope.
I would keep my private script all to myself—
at least try to, anyway.
Maybe the really bad grammar
and punctuation would improve.
And my sensibilities would outstrip
the ones I have now. That would be cool.
That would be the way I would look at it,
I hope.
Then come back six years later
and really try hard again.
I know more than I did six years ago,
and express it infinitely better,
especially in the written form.
It would be hard to abandon the hope of progression
and accept abject failure all at once.
At least not lose any of it, even if it isn't that good!

In a Frightful Now

I hope you can tolerate someone
not so thought out as you.
Foolish men and women
are certainly not new to you.
Don't think I implied that.
I understand completely the sweeps
you've made up through society.
The stench of poison exists
as well as appetizing scents.
I'll go further.
I think you are keenly aware of
illogic and violence, especially,
as you embody their opposites.
I am a little rough around the edges though.

My Nature

Boppin your head to the funk that is not there,
with the teeth and lip making the "F" sound face,
two thumbs pointing at yourself,
saying audibly, "Ugh."
Almost every thought of it,
me being with you,
appeals to my ego,
as well as to my animal side.
I would like it so much.
The thought that it would result in
almost immediate regret on your part,
and dwindling affections from then on,
to result in dislike,
is devastating.

That breaks down all the strong walls.

Crash

If you could return 10%
of the affection I have for you,
I would be satisfied,
totally satisfied.
However, knowing that you've retained
only 90% of the impact,
almost makes me almost want total rejection from you,
so that you would feel the full force of it.
I guess it would just be in that interval
before you told me of your disinterest,
that you would feel that 100%.
Maybe a kind word would be in order though.
It might slow me down a mile per hour or two.

Loneliness

Baby, you're in your man's apartment,
watching a baseball game on television,
eating Campbell's soup.
You're about as American as you can get.
You know (most of the time) introspection
is the biggest lie of all.

Nausea

I will find my cave. That is my mission.
I can't be exposed to the this anymore.
I can't just say *no* anymore; because
inaction is now somehow

action-like in its inactivity.
Thank God there are other places!

Keeping

I am trying something very difficult at my age,
attempting to learn something brand new.
Not at me leisure, but hurried, running in fast.
I convince myself my successes are morphing
confidence onto my face,
while I butcher a subtle craft.

Letting It Slide

I am very lower class.
Maybe you don't think,
my thinking should be so influenced by that.
Sorry, that's the way it is.
One of the prime thoughts,
after only a few years of lower class laboring,
is not what to do, but what not to do.
With no exception, I have been expected
to do the absolute impossible
on barely survivable wages.
I'm sure it's better here than anywhere else.
That doesn't make good, though,
and don't expect me to be happy about it.

Michaux

I think the forced sharing of honest feelings
would leave me at a total disadvantage.
I don't recognize virtues

such as honesty in my feelings.
Some things make me happy only sometimes.
I would be forced to reveal different honest feelings
about the same issue at different times.
Pick and choose the ones that suit you.
But I revealed that to you. This makes me happy.
It must be true.
And down you go.
Unfortunately, so far away from
the human experience of happiness,
as to be almost irretrievable.
(The irony—it is not something
most people would want anyway.
I'm afraid real, inner, primal happiness,
probably involves the killing of small animals.)
It's a good way to rid someone
of their personality though—
at least at the house.
No, thank you.
I'm not giving up on the idea,
that there is something else in the world:
Fully developed individuals,
that are going to disagree
about almost everything.
The urge to mate
has a promise of happiness implied,
but in the end, it is just mating.
Advanced people make the best of it.
We share a fate,
let's be witty about it.
A teasing put down
gives energy to your individuality.

And when your thumping around
in another room,
I vow to have two conflicting thoughts—
I wonder what you're doing
and I couldn't care less.
Beyond the formality of social cues,
we are always in the present when it's just us.
Which is not really that great,
but it is the best under the circumstances.

A Little Salaried Man

How many different ways can I talk about shit?
It seems endless.
I used to fancy myself a writer.
In no other avenue of artistic expression,
did I have anything but a trace of talent.
I met you and learned about your art stuff.
How you were a patron—
understood it.
I started writing again.

Hygiene

This has both positive and negative implications,
results, that is—
the states of mind so created.
But you say,
"The candidate must be psychologically cleared."
A shaman so oppressed once remarked,
"Take half the world. At night we dream.
At dawn we awaken still."

Hint Hint

I always doubted a relationship
being an organic thing,
but this comes close.
Your guilt and your pride
waiver back and forth,
making you act in certain ways.
And my lust and low self esteem
are responding and integrating with them.
These four states of mind
are now interacting on purpose.
I don't really need to describe
the fuel for this machine—
anything.
This relationship has a covalent bond.
The organic things (us) are there too.
We're just buzzing around the matrix though.
Giving up a little bit of ourselves to stay attached.
Just a little bit.
If one of us were a painter,
the surrealism of it would be expressed.

Eleven A.M.

The streets of Seattle are charming.
I like when they are dry and dusty
just as much as when overflowing with puddles.
I don't see gleaming facades
on idle robin's egg weekdays.
Nor do I see edifices in ivy
with reliefs cutting through the gloom.
Sometimes I smell those things

(cut grass and mold),
but haven't seen them since I was fifteen.
Since then, whenever a rolling hill or a vista
is presented to my downward gaze,
which feature scenery such as these,
I feel I must fall into it,
so I step all the way to the edge
and look all the way down.
I cannot look at it.

Butt-head Poetry

There's lots of trees and stuff
outside my window.

The Dollars, the Art, and the Love

I don't blame him in the least
for being so jealous.
But don't single me out,
it was a team effort.
They were looking for the best writer,
and used all kinds of skills to deliver
that author's work to their devoted readers,
who received a quality product
at a reasonable price.
I think the whole scheme was good.

Status Piecemeal

How could these two people even meet?
I'm sorry, unless they grew up together,
were neighbors or something,

it is not plausible.
Two shy people don't end up with each other;
they are alone or abused.

Facts

Dorothy injured her head in the whirlwind.
Oz was a frenzy cooked up in her head.
Dorothy is supposed to be eleven.
In Oz, she's bigger than everyone else
and more real.
When she wakes up, it is sad.

It May Be Tears

Just always think this,
I am the greatest guy in the world,
and you're the greatest gal.
Anything that would happen
and I would act appropriately.
It may not be *reality*,
and it would certainly be bad drama,
but it would be appropriate.

Guilty

Being oversensitive it would hurt.
But even if you betrayed me, I would move on.
That is, if you'd let me.
You may see fit to torture me as well.
Have me whipped and flayed—
almost every nerve ending raw,
continuously beaten,

Then you may then come up close
(make sure the eyes are unharmed),
and face my shiny, quivering body,
and my insane mind,
and knife my heart.

This

Excluding fanciful imaginings,
this is absolutely the best
things could possibly have turned out.
I am going to put this plainly—
it is undeniable that without you,
this would not have happened.
I am not minimizing my own achievement,
nor the good fortune of my employer
who granted me this opportunity
in this whole hiring process.
But you,
who combines true good will
for your fellow human beings,
with the respect you must have felt
for my talent and intelligence—
I have to single you out.
You gauged the reality of the world
which fails to see merit so often.
And you convinced me that most minds
are unmanageable to the idea
of necessity and weakness.
When it comes to things like this—
new beginnings, learning,
"Necessity and weakness is what is called for."

Icebreaker

I think we are both here on this site
for the same general purpose,
to be a couple.
I am here to find a hot girlfriend.
And you are totally willing
to put up with someone not so hot,
so long as he has at least
something going on his life.

Couples

There are couples (both doctors)
whose biggest challenge in life
are reminders about pocket-protectors and crumbs.
Of this population,
surely there must be psychoanalysts as a subset.
I salute you.
You're objective enough.
Emotions that break through the vault door
must have outside and inside help.

Cheering

When Hulk Hogan used to win a match,
he would go to each side of the ring
with his hand to his ear.
Which side would be the loudest?
He would narrow it down to two,
and then the winning side.
That side gets its reward, Hulkamania flexes.
He is their trophy.

Disease Vector

No one is feeling real happiness right now.
They can't be.
Because if they are,
they are beneath contempt
being so satisfied with something
so crushingly unsatisfying,
whatever it is.
Or maybe they are.

Porging

Sure, some is dandruff
fallen on the parchment,
but most people want revealed
how disappointing they are to God,
they along with everyone else—
especially everyone else.
That is a good sermon.
I see myself in there too.
I will sit for this.

But Outside

I cannot face what I am.
It is too terrible.
It is too obvious.
I wrestle against this,
and am infected with the sweat of it.
Sinews stretch,
joints extend and bend—
all this against me.

A saving grace—
no smiles from the gloom.
Not a confronting champion,
a terrible one.

Abs

It won't be anything girlfriend-y,
don't worry about that.
I know you have your creep-meter
tuned to the male frequency.
You like to see emotions displayed in art.
Even though it seems a natural selection,
politics just doesn't go into it well.
The awe does not vortex inside,
it's more like peritonitis.

More News from the Community

"A friend of mine," he continued,
"is an outdoorsman to a religious,
non-religious, degree.
But he gets lost—
sometimes at least.
He says he cannot trust his mind out there.
He thinks it's some kind of biologic file dump.
(He's in IT.)
He says he populates the forest.
He interprets these episodes himself.
I'm probably the only person he has let in on it.
He went into detail with only one episode.
It was tactile.
Citizens aren't seen where he goes,

where he needs to go—
a vacuum.
His last rational memory
is always stillness and footsteps.
This time it was windy.
The trees absorbing and chopping up the wind,
Preventing it from affecting
his stability in the bedlam.
In a clearing, he saw a woodshed.
That was not rational.
And a man weeping,
sitting on a stump,
soaking his bushy brown beard.
He said he walked up and touched it."
Everything by observation?
I can tell you that is not true.
Animism meant something:
Already infused with instinct,
attributing that quality
to other animals and plants,
and making a thing out of it.

Don't Fight It

A language improves, not declines.
Words are in the public domain.
If a word, once narrowly defined,
becomes commonly used for another concept,
even if that concept was specifically excluded
in the original definition,
it is the judgment of the speakers of that language
that there is no distinction between them in reality.

Good Luck Ignoring It

I don't think our forebears
thought much of big rocks.
One of many.
One of many.
When someone crawled all over it,
and carved a face out of it,
that was different.
That would be a place to come back to.
You can't take it with you,
or bash it in.

Bread Basket

Go somewhere like Kansas,
where there are no sides only safe,
while the worst of humanity rules the rest—
thin themselves out.

Art Walk

We don't harm anyone.
Why take that beauty away?
"But must it be grafted to gutters?
Or spread sheets?
Please, it is not a donor site."
But we did graft it ourselves, didn't we?
A carpenter's level, keystroke, and mouse—
productivity and function stylized,
just to get through the day.
I need the nonsense.

Stable

Joan of Arc on an early Spring campaign,
that picture of you in the snow
wearing leather and fur,
looking trapped in the forest
but indifferent.
The torch awaits.
Your face alight, transcendent, totally tapped in.
The pyre is a candle.
Every day is a better person,
the day before grown forward.
A lesson from the farm.
Everything dies—
another lesson.
And everything the priest tells you is true.
The news he tells you is so.

Unstable

I am eviscerating this hillside.
Every warrior that comes upon me
I overcome and kill, every civilian too.
I slaughter all people, nothing left of the seed.
I burn everything, not even a memory left.
Then take a two-week vacation—
all the time thinking about cutting throats,
piercing vitals, caving in heads, and no pity.
I have destroyed many nations.
It is a small number compared to
the number that I will. I can't wait for it!
Beheadings, crushing ribcages, stabbing groins!
"When the homo sapiens discovers

it cannot dominate the vast majority
of its peers, it dominates concepts
and disciplines in isolation.
(This is static and defining.)
The range of neuroses
is roughly the same and surprisingly
proportional to what it has always been.
(In this respect, regression.)
Sadistic pleasure and honor
each motivates two subsets
of humanity, and these in turn
motivate society.
(Static.)
The universities try to
meld the two in the same person,
to underwhelming success."

Alarm

That is not a deal. Morning or not,
I want my tongue
to touch every square inch of your mouth.
The more we know that,
the more expressed the feeling.

Confirmation Bias

The fear of existence is the fear of
ingestion in the garden of Eden.
When compared with the world unrulable,
I would be afraid.
It makes sense to me.
Like the hairs of men

this earth is continually covered.
And inside are just as many depravities,
it's called nature.
Spare in spots, thank God,
where you can see where you walk—
bitten so many times, your ankles have gravitas.
This respite will give you
a chance to clear your throat
and express out loud your elderly wisdom
about living in this history,
of the imbecilic nature of mankind,
about becoming history,
about the endless circuit through generations,
brutal overthrows, savage defense,
and endless pain before and after,
and constantly pregnant.
Remind the boys and girls.
Just how much sinks in and is incorporated?
How long these things take!
Kept in for so long,
this auto-obituary will be heard.

Fear

I think my room will prefer the darkness.
Light only reveals the logic, happiness, and safety
erupting wart-like out of my face
away from civilization.

It's Not Fear

Believe me, I know what's going on.
People are concerned about me on many levels.

I completely understand all these issues.
Personality? Not social to a pathological degree?
But I'm happy.
Yes, circumstances more than anything else
have determined my condition,
but there were many willful acts
mixed in there, too, that I do not regret.
And I have learned to live this way very well.
Every other way would be struggle for me.
(At my age? Wouldn't you have to agree with that?)
So success on my rehabilitation
from social isolation
would be a wooden, role playing fantasy.
No, thank you!
I think I have answered a secondary concern
by telling you that at many key points in my life,
I consciously chose to be alone
when that seemed to be my only escape.
Realize, though, that I also
consciously chose to put myself
in those situations
that I would subsequently opt out of.
Thus, sometimes I willfully don't do things
that a part of me really wants to do.
But I do make considered decisions.
Don't take it personally if I decide
not to respond the way I know you want me to.
I think it's better for the both of us when I don't.

Stoning

I've been looking through

this thread, and it's pretty clear
to me who is a member of the
Mean Girls' Club, and it's not
to whom it's dedicated.

Fodder

I address these same committed
soberly and directly,
fact four—
there is no plan of retreat.

Tread Lightly

Well, I think if we're supposed
to be non-trainees in a trainee atmosphere,
we should be paid that way too.
We are obviously not.
Or, on the other hand,
we are exactly who our badges say we are,
and an allowance should be made,
or at least faked.
I don't respond well to drill sergeant motivation—
fair warning.

Coffee

I know I lack the big three—
looks, style, and money.
I've been trying find a woman, right now,
who's young enough to have a child with me.
Anyway, on the other hand,
or foot, as we walk away from each other,

these complexes we have are so primal and basic,
that I feel satisfied.
It is as if we exchanged genetic material.

A Heart Encrypted, Unwilling to Share

"He cannot will himself out of death.
It mocks him to the grave.
That conquest would logically have
to come from the nihilistic sterilization
of its prey—death must die.
The only answer is an impossible one."
That was it. The crying stopped too.
Then I heard stapling and collating.

(The Title)

Whether or not the extent
of my mental health condition
has been misrepresented
is not important to me.
The state of my mental health
is none of your fucking business.
If that is what you crave,
intimate connection with the author,
I suggest the "Real World".
If you want documented footage
of how I felt when I was betrayed,
when I first realized I was ugly,
with no future, no money,
no girlfriend, no hope,
I can't help you.
I am following the tradition

of most tribes everywhere—
having the person deal with these things
mostly on their own.
It's certainly not open for general discussion.
When it is revealed, it emerges
a lot of time in the form of art,
which is what I have tried to accomplish here.
And which I certainly hope to foster in society,
not to drown as an unwanted child.

Dinner Theater

Let's face it, some of this shit
is way off base and ignorant,
and some of it is brilliant.
Deal with it.
I and others like me
are just trying to sell
human stories
about the human mind.
It is not supposed to be for all time,
just for the time being.
It does not resonate today
the grunting tale
of the exploits of the tribe
that we've just defeated,
and perhaps eaten,
but I'm sure it brought
tears to everyone's eyes back then.
And I think it promotes togetherness
and not division—
something those apart can truly appreciate.

Neo

The constellations have changed.
Existence has changed also in our eyes.
Our evolving minds,
reinforced through the generations,
are becoming more prominently acute.
The casual understanding, so humble,
but not too far remote,
which made up for its gaps in knowledge
with the notion of omnipresence,
has been so fine-tuned to causation
that an almost complete
cosmology has been described.

Hiding?

I asked you that question about romance,
and it was very difficult for you to answer.
Like when I was grilled (I said it)
about my past relationships,
and the reasons for their ends.
There is a lot I don't want to admit about that.
I always try to improve.
It doesn't excuse the lack of effort
to resuscitate, I know.
But I do excel at improvement and new starts.
It's not all bad.
I don't think you were hiding.
It might be a physical thing,
or rather an embarrassment
to admit something about a physical thing,
something that is directly related to romance,

that is the difficulty for you.
Like when I repress (I said it)
that I never really physically satisfy anyone I'm with.
I think it is a neuromuscular syndrome—
a hair trigger and an endless supply of testosterone.
Some, I'm positive,
suffer from the hypo- of this syndrome; there is
little or no
physical romantic sensations felt at all.
"This is just an arrangement for a visa.
But a solemn one that will be honored—
what else do you want?"
I think you can improve.
I think there is a basic thing
that you are not experiencing.
I'll tell you what,
I'll buy Redbook online or something,
and get all kinds of good ideas about things:
"What to Do to Make Your Partner Feel Special".
I'm sure at least some of them will hit the mark.
(Needless to say, it will work on me.)
I won't overdo it, though, don't worry.
I will utilize the calendar on my phone
to schedule my thoughtfulness.
How's that?
And you can help me out too.

Night Watch

I tire.
I sometimes dream of you.
A couple more jumps closer to the wood

and obscurity.
Soft carpets, fabric wallpaper,
accent lighting, fruity smelling—
the mist and fog descends from the ceiling.
We have a need for the perfect dance partner.
We have a need for mischief.
And being so good at that…
Biological cells dividing—
tingling, creative,
evoking emotion,
primal,
spreading tissue.

Cold War

I think it's January.
No matter,
burning a bunch of stuff will solve everything.

Bustling

A lodge, a hall, even a bar,
on a raw November seven PM,
and doors bursting in with brightness
and neon and sweat,
foosball, laughing, speeches—
it all just make me feel so unwelcome.
There is nothing that can be done about that.

Recovery

Okay, let's see if I can remember
some of this shit.

I worked seven hours
and got paid for eight.
(I'll forgo an analysis of that.
I don't want to get sidetracked.)
My focus is on the basics of it—
the bus, the routine, that stuff.
I used to think about that kind of thing all the time.
A memory exercise if nothing else.
But primarily because I think
I'm probably going to have to start
doing that shit again.
I won't be as fit,
or as quick
(that's a cinch).
Will it be too much for me?
Will this be where the will to live ends?
If so, merely a memory exercise.
The basics—
trash, vacuuming, bathrooms, breakrooms—
just easy does it.
The bus?
No.
That's not going to happen.
Please.
Night shift/graveyard busses?
No.
I would seriously despair.
Just going to have to get junker after junker.
I'm sure I caught a bus around 11:30 to go home.
Did we start at four?
Yes.
Because I mopped that deli's floor

just when they were closing,
and emptied their garbage.
I worked in two buildings.
The other was four blocks south.
I spent roughly 60% of the time in one
And 40% in the other.
I think the majority was spent in that other one.
But I just can't remember!
What did I do there?
One floor and the stairs—
sales, Y2K software, 1998...
There were five floors.
Which one was mine?
(God, catching a bus on Westlake or Dexter
At 11:45? Today?
Fuck.)
I vacuumed the three elevator lobbies too.
I peeked in at the cars one day.
Felt like I was trespassing.
Room numbers?
Views?
Yes. I saw the flash grenades during WTO
looking southeast to downtown.
Don't remember looking out at the views much.
Wow, I was straight back then.
Head down and work.
Never hardly ran into anyone,
except my fellow janitors—
I saw one of them after, a year or so later!
Both of them—just ran into them!
How about that!
Which floor was it?

No Basis in Reality

I came early on Christmas Eve
and New Year's Eve—
the people seemed like so many.
Just a fraction of the call center's capacity though.
Conference rooms? No.
The kitchenette in the middle,
that guy that always worked late (closer?),
the punk rock girl with all the pics in her cube,
all the plants in the atrium,
and the management's office…
What else?
Black holes.
The division of labor to sell software—
didn't have a clue.
Made schematics of plug-in routes
for the vacuuming.
Would go over key words in it (names?)
as I went along.
I would also have the same song
(different one each day)
going on in my head all night long.
It is in my mind,
or at least a derivative of it,
because I know if I went back to it somehow,
Doctor Who-like, I would pick up on it quickly.
It's frustrating,
I can't bring it to the surface.
It is key to remembering my schedule,
my routine.
I started at four.
Caught a bus at 50th and Latona.
It took me twenty minutes to walk to that bus stop.

And I reckon the trip to Westlake
was, let's say, twenty minutes.
Did I hang out before shift?
I didn't smoke. At least not at first.
Could we just start?
I remember David was late once,
on a Sunday,
two days after
that bus plunged off the Aurora bridge,
and we had to wait for him.
The bus gets there when it's supposed to get there.
I caught it at 3:30.
I left home at 3:00.
It was Sunday to Thursday.
Paying back the government around this time too.
Paid them back in full,
with interest.
The daughter of the family that ran the deli
was there once on a Sunday, too,
with her boyfriend—
probably after some church function.
They were holding hands as they left.
I have such a poor sense of proportion.
Doctor Who-like my brain would just fry
walking down some of those corridors.

High Council

I don't harm anyone.
In this day and age,
isn't that the golden rule?
I know it would be a cause of concern

in an advanced but still humble stage.
"Why does he laugh
Then?
Why is he there
Now?
Why does this happen?
Parents?
Some game is weaker, dumber…"
It is definitely not wanted.
It will be eliminated
and any known line.

Hell No

I don't know, but I would think
that there must be some kind of bio-ethic
that would rule out your approach.
For a very optional form of treatment
the clinician shall not enter into a debate
about it with the patient.

Leilani Estates

It's condos and decks,
boyfriends, girlfriends,
deck furniture.
beautiful picture windows,
views on two sides,
a lake and a park.
It doesn't matter what the subject matter is,
it is going to be intimidating.
I don't know the basic scams.
That is the main problem,

total ignorance.

Not Cool

I am not even aware of my body.
Is that a familiar burning sensation or atypical?
I should keep a better inventory of symptoms.
Presenting myself
as some sort of prize
to your notice.
I know I can turn it on
like a waterfall
neon sign.

Inspiration

Do you have a plan when you enter a pub?
It's just the same.
I may haunt a corner for a season
because I am impressive and derive pleasure.
I will give it every chance,
but I will move on.
It's just like that.

Low Self-Opinion?

Wrong. So wrong.
I purposely self-deprecate.
And for a couple of very good reasons.
The first is, I don't want to seem conceited.
I know how great I am,
I have to guard against
showing pride about it though.

That is virtuous.
Second, it deflects the piercing blow
of actually being wrong.
I have excellent timing for my over-dramatic
apologizing, and court statements.
I credit that to this humor.
This behavior is the result of considered decisions.

Grime

Let's live the life of a confident man.
Walk down alleys,
hear the hollow sounds of glass
and chinaware clanging,
and industrial hoses (spotless).
I am confident.
I know kitchen routine.
Anything out of place?
Walk as quietly as possible,
but purposefully and confidently,
totally ready to gut someone.
I meet new people here,
have business—
God, all the cameras!
I will be vulnerable from Union
to the Battery Street Tunnel.
And be all alone the whole time.
All the way to my car.
I know which places have bartenders
who would deflect pursuers if it came to that:
"Someone just went out the back way…"
I know which friends are in which buildings,

men and women,
who would be happy to put me up.
I will totally get away with this—
but on the bus, tomorrow morning.
Lounge about while others bother.
Showing gratitude for the hospitality.
And enjoying a gracious host.
My schedule will start again tomorrow—
light contemporary classical music until then,
and white carpets,
and pianos,
and being loved.

There Needs to Be a Mate

I like to think of it as a trick.
I am immensely attracted to androgynous women,
and modest ones,
who dress like they lack sexual characteristics.
I am conscious of this as a fact.
The trick comes in because
I think those hips are more attractive,
and breasts sexier—
and they're not,
no worse, no better,
pretty much exactly the same.
I think my mind tricks me,
this is a more sensible choice,
for whatever reason.
And here I am confronted by you.
You are incredibly feminine—
sculpted.

on purpose,
the best—
heat.
For some reason, it is the same kind of love.
And when I stare into your face,
so pretty,
the beautiful blonde curls phase out,
and I almost see a man,
a professional man,
a respected one.
I think my mind is at it again…
She is okay.

Sometimes Clueless

I know you've just met me,
and this might be a hard claim to live up to,
but there are very few human beings that I dislike.
And it's not in me to be intentionally mean—
even to them.
I'm not polished though.
A text may seem rude.
I usually catch those and add,
"That didn't come out right."

Cape Cod

Hi, Jordan,
I am having a fantasy about you right now.
I have imagined you a famous woman,
Katherine Hepburn.
I'm seeing you, though, when you're older,
going over your life with a young

(pretty herself) biographer.
And talking about all your romances!
Your men!
There is no doubt that I would rank last
in sophistication and impact on the world.
Only the name Robby is what remains of me.
(Noticing you've stopped at the name,
she repeats it.)

Greenhouse

For some reason, the asparagus is doing well.
"Who planted that?"
That thing? We don't know.
It must have come with the soil,
or someone brought a salad in here.
"A common garden vegetable
in with these lovelies—
it's almost quaint."

www.ingramcontent.com/pod-product-compliance
Lightning Source LLC
Chambersburg PA
CBHW031122080526
44587CB00011B/1079